**Art Revelations**

Sean Connolly

# NEW TESTAMENT MIRACLES

ENCHANTED LION BOOKS
NEW YORK

First American Edition published in 2004 by
Enchanted Lion Books
115 West 18th Street, 6th floor, New York, NY, 10011
Copyright © 2004 McRae Books Srl
All rights reserved
Printed and bound in Belgium

The series "Art Revelations"
was created and produced by McRae Books Srl
Borgo Santa Croce, 8 – Florence (Italy)
info@mcraebooks.com

Art History consultant: Roberto Carvalho de Magalhães
Text: Sean Connolly
Illustrations: Studio Stalio (Alessandro Cantucci,
Fabiano Fabbrucci, Andrea Morandi)
Graphic Design: Marco Nardi
Picture Research and editing: Loredana Agosta
Layout: Studio Yotto

Library of Congress Cataloging-in-Publication Data
Connolly, Sean, 1956–
  New Testament miracles / Sean Connolly, – 1st American ed.
    p. cm – (Art revelations)
  Includes index.
  Summary: Presents brief retellings of the miracles of Jesus Christ, accompanied by paintings by eminent artists from the past and details about each work.
  ISBN 1-59270-012-8
  1. Jesus Christ–Miracles–Art–Juvenile literature. 2. Bible. N.T.–Illustrations–Juvenile literature. 3. Miracles in art–Juvenile literature. [1. Jesus Christ–Miracles–Art. 2. Miracles in art. 3. Bible stories–N.T.–Illustrations.] I. Title. II Series.

N8051.C66 2004
226.7'09505–dc22
                                                                    2004049414

*opposite bottom:* MASOLINO DA PANICALE (AND MASACCIO),
*Healing of the Cripple and Raising of Tabitha,*
Brancacci Chapel, Santa Maria del Carmine, Florence

*previous page:* PETER PAUL RUBENS,
*The Rockox Triptych (central panel),*
Koninklijk Museum voor Schone Kunsten, Antwerp

# Table of contents

Introduction   4

Jesus Heals the Leper   6

The Centurion's Servant   8

Jesus Calms the Sea   10

The Pool of Bethesda   12

Multiplication of the Loaves and Fishes   14

Jesus Heals a Man Born Blind   16

The Raising of Lazarus   18

The Healing of a Boy with a Demon   20

The Haul of Fish   22

The Descent of the Holy Spirit   24

Peter   26

The Conversion of Paul   28

A Chronology of Miracles / Artists' Biographies   30

Index   32

# Introduction

*Jesus went throughout Galilee, teaching in their synagogues, preaching the good news of the kingdom, and healing every disease and sickness among the people. News about him spread all over Syria, and people brought to him all who were ill with various diseases, those suffering severe pain, the demon-possessed, those having seizures, and the paralyzed, and he healed them.*   Matthew 4:23–25

The Bible recounts many miracles, or events that suspend the normal laws of nature. For the Jews, Old Testament miracles such as the parting of the Red Sea were signs of God's power to intervene on behalf of his people. Jesus, in the New Testament, constantly equates his miracles with faith. The faithful — those who are willing to heed Jesus and follow his teachings — are the people who benefit from the miracles. Those who witness them spread Jesus' word, drawing more faithful to his message.

*This Greek icon shows Jesus with his right hand raised in blessing, as he is often depicted in images of his miracles.*

### THE MINISTRY OF JESUS

The four evangelists — Matthew, Mark, Luke, and John — devote most of their writings to the last three years of Jesus' life, ending with his crucifixion in Jerusalem. During that time, following his baptism by John the Baptist at the age of 30, Jesus traveled in and around his native region of Galilee, preaching, gathering disciples, and performing miracles. Many of these miracles occurred by the Sea of Galilee or in towns such as Capernaum which lay along its shores.

*This detail from a medieval mosaic shows Jesus healing a blind man by touching the man's eyes.*

### HEALING MIRACLES

Jesus performed two types of miracle. The first, usually described as "nature miracles," included the miracle of the loaves and fishes (pages 14–15) and his walking on water (page 16). These showed Jesus' divine power. The second type, of which there were many more, involved healing people of ailments and physical disabilities. They include the accounts of the leper (see pages 6–7), the blind man (pages 20–21), and most dramatically, Lazarus (pages 18–19). Jesus stressed that it was the faith of these people that healed them. Each miracle underlines Jesus' insistence that people maintain their faith in God as revealed through his teachings.

THE MIRACLES OF JESUS
*Roman art*
c. 450–60
Victoria & Albert Museum, London (UK)

This ivory panel depicting six of Jesus' miracles was carved in Rome about 130 years after Christianity was adopted by the Romans as the state religion, and about the time that the Empire fell to invading Germanic and Slavic peoples. The scenes show (1) the miracle of the loaves and fishes (see pages 14–15); (2) Jesus raising Lazarus (see pages 18–19); (3) Jesus healing the blind man (see pages 16–17); (4) Jesus changing water into wine at the wedding feast at Cana; (5) the paralyzed man carrying away his mat after being cured at the Pool of Bethesda (pages 12–13); (6) the leper being cured by Jesus (see pages 6–7).

### JESUS AND HIS APOSTLES

Jesus gained many disciples, or followers. The 12 disciples who became closest to Jesus, accompanying him on many of his travels and later charged with spreading his message, are known as the apostles. Jesus gave these men the power to perform miracles as well, so that they could also preach the message of redemption — or healing — through faith in Jesus. The New Testament records that "many signs and wonders were being done by the apostles." The miracles performed by the apostles had much the same effect as those of Jesus: they gained many new followers but they also put the apostles at great risk from the same authorities who had ordered Jesus' crucifixion.

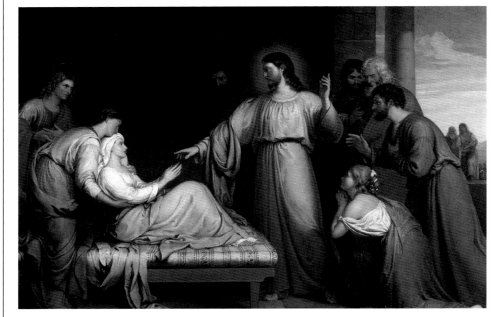

*The 19th-century British painter John Bridges depicted Jesus curing Peter's mother-in-law of a fever while Peter watches from the right.*

# Jesus Heals the Leper

*When he came down from the mountainside, large crowds followed him. A man with leprosy came and knelt before him and said "Lord, if you are willing, you can make me clean." Jesus reached out his hand and touched the man. "I am willing," he said. "Be clean." Immediately he was cured of his leprosy.*     Matthew 8:1–3

Jewish law had strict restrictions about leprosy, which left sufferers with running sores, and even led to the loss of fingers and toes. Priests would judge whether a person had the disease, isolating the sufferer from the community until he or she recovered. Having healed the leper, Jesus urged him to keep quiet and report to a priest. In doing so, Jesus was showing that he was working within existing Jewish law and not trying to overturn it. However, the man did talk freely, and word of Jesus' power spread quickly. Jesus could no longer enter a town openly and pray silently in "lonely places."

*Many medieval paintings highlighted the open sores and pathetic expressions of lepers in biblical times.*

*Like many other artists depicting the Sermon on the Mount, the Florentine Fra Angelico (c. 1400–1455) shows Jesus seated. This posture links Jesus with other Jewish leaders, who traditionally sat while they taught.*

### JESUS BEGINS TO PREACH AND HEAL THE SICK

Soon after recruiting the first four of his 12 apostles – Simon Peter, Andrew, James, and John – Jesus entered the town of Capernaum and went to the synagogue to teach. A man called out "What do you want with us, Jesus of Nazareth? Have you come to destroy us? I know who you are: the Holy One of God." Jesus saw that the man was possessed by a demon, which he ordered to be silent. It took an evil spirit to recognize Jesus for who he was, but the astounded onlookers saw to it that Jesus' reputation quickly spread.

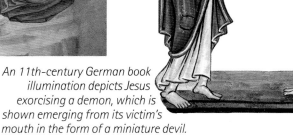

*An 11th-century German book illumination depicts Jesus exorcising a demon, which is shown emerging from its victim's mouth in the form of a miniature devil.*

### THE BEATITUDES

Jesus left Capernaum and went to a nearby hillside. Large crowds gathered, either to be healed or simply to hear the message of the new kingdom. Jesus' words are recalled as the Sermon on the Mount. It is Jesus' announcement of the coming of the kingdom, and it contains a series of demands for Jesus' followers. The Sermon begins with promises of blessings for those who belong to the kingdom. Together these promises are known as the *Beatitudes*, from the Latin word *beatus*, or "blessed." Having shown his followers the rewards for the blessed, Jesus called on his followers to "turn the other cheek" to evildoers and be discreet about giving to the poor. The Sermon ended with several parables on the theme of the coming judgement.

### SERMON ON THE MOUNT AND HEALING OF THE LEPER
*Cosimo Rosselli*
1481
Sistine Chapel, Vatican City

In this work the Florentine artist Cosimo Rosselli (1439–1507), probably aided by his pupil Piero di Cosimo (1462–1521), showed two biblical accounts — the Sermon on the Mount and the Healing of the Leper — in one work of art. In this reproduction of the right half of the fresco, we see Jesus (1) surrounded by the apostles (2) as the pious leper (3) kneels before him. In the background, we can see Jesus and the disciples coming down from the mountain after the Sermon (4). This scene links the two parts of the painting.

## JESUS AND THE CENTURION
*Paolo Veronese*
c. 1571
Prado, Madrid (Spain)

In this painting by the Venetian artist Paolo Veronese (1528–88), the centurion (1) is kneeling before Jesus (2). The centurion has removed his helmet which is held by a page (3). Jesus is surrounded by some of his disciples (4) while the centurion is accompanied by a group of centuries (Roman soldiers) (5).

## THE WIDOW OF NAIN

Some time after healing the centurion's servant Jesus arrived at the town of Nain accompanied by his disciples and a large crowd. At the town gate he saw a funeral procession. The only son of a widow was about to be buried, and the people were carrying the body on a bier. Jesus was overcome with pity for the woman. He touched the bier and said to the corpse, "Young man, I tell you: get up." At that moment the man sat up and started speaking. The astonished crowd began hailing Jesus as a prophet.

*This detail of a 1 4th-century Serbian mural shows the widow's son, still bound for burial, sitting up on the funeral bier.*

# The Centurion's Servant

*When Jesus entered Capernaum, a centurion came to him, asking for help. "Lord," he said, "my servant lies at home paralyzed and in terrible suffering." Jesus said to him, "I will go and heal him." The centurion replied, "Lord, I do not deserve to have you come under my roof. But just say the word, and my servant will be healed."* Matthew 8:5–8

Jesus' healing of the centurion's servant appears in the gospels of Matthew and Luke. It is the first instance of Jesus using his powers to benefit a Gentile (non-Jewish person). Jesus saw himself as a Jew working and preaching within the Jewish tradition. His willingness to help a Gentile — and a Roman at that — is significant. The centurion, for his part, respects Jewish culture and knows that it would be an act of impurity for Jesus to enter his house. For this reason he asks that Jesus simply say the word — that and the centurion's own faith would be enough to heal the servant.

### A GENTILE'S FAITH
In Jesus' time the Holy Land was part of the Roman Empire. The principal unit of the Roman army was the legion, with 6,000 soldiers divided into 60 centuries (100 soldiers). Centurions, known for their loyalty and dependability, commanded the centuries. The centurion in this story knows the value of obedience and understands that Jesus' word — like his own to the troops — will be enough. Jesus is amazed by this faith, which is greater than any he had come across in Israel.

*This detail of a Roman relief shows Roman soldiers in battle regalia, with swords, shields, and the standard. The centurion would have commanded just such a group.*

### JESUS CURES A PARALYTIC
When Jesus returned to Capernaum a second time, a great crowd gathered inside and around the house where he was staying. A group of four men arrived, carrying a paralyzed friend on a stretcher. They climbed onto the roof, stripped it away and lowered their friend toward Jesus. Recognizing this faith, Jesus said, "Son, your sins are forgiven." This showed the link that Jews made between sin and disability. Some Jewish teachers who were present considered this statement blasphemous because only God can forgive sins. Jesus told them that it would have been easier simply to have cured the man than to forgive his sins. Then, to show that he could do both, Jesus ordered the paralyzed man to get up. To the astonishment of the crowd, the man walked away.

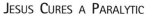

*A 6th-century mosaic in Ravenna's church of Sant'Apollinare Nuovo vividly depicts the paralyzed man being lowered through the roof into the house where Jesus is preaching.*

# Jesus Calms the Sea

*A furious squall came up, and the waves broke over the boat, so that it was nearly swamped. Jesus was in the stern, sleeping on a cushion. The disciples woke him and said to him, "Teacher, don't you care if we drown?" He got up, rebuked the wind and said to the waves, "Quiet! Be still!" Then the wind died down and was completely calm. He said to his disciples, "Why are you so afraid? Do you still have no faith?"* Mark 4:37–41

THE STORM ON THE SEA OF GALILEE
*Rembrandt Harmenszoon van Rijn*
1633
Whereabouts unknown; previously Isabella Stewart Gardner Museum, Boston (USA), stolen 1990

This dramatic painting by Rembrandt (1606–69) vividly portrays the intensity of the storm, with Jesus (1), calmly seated at the stern of the boat surrounded by the disciples who have just woken him (2). The other disciples are struggling with the sail and riggings, trying desperately to control the boat (3). Adding a touch of realism, Rembrandt has shown one disciple being sick over the side (4). Christian painters often used the boat as a symbol of the Church. Here the Church is held on course under the calm eye of Jesus.

The Sea of Galilee is actually a freshwater lake, now known as Lake Tiberius, in northern Israel. A huge crowd had gathered as Jesus preached by the shores of the lake, forcing Jesus and his disciples to board a boat and continue preaching from the water. At day's end Jesus suggested that they cross to the other side and along the way a sudden storm developed. The disciples were terrified, but Jesus had fallen asleep. Wakened by the disciples' cries, he rebuked both the wind and the disciples for their lack of faith. The miracle showed that Jesus could calm storms – both actual and the metaphoric "storms" people face in their lives.

*This 12th-century mosaic from St. Mark's Basilica in Venice, shows Jesus twice: first asleep at the stern (right) and later standing with outstretched arm as he calms the sea.*

### THE HEALING OF THE DEMON-POSSESSED MAN

After calming the storm, Jesus and his disciples landed on the eastern side on the Sea of Galilee in a place known as Gadarenes. As Jesus stepped from the boat he met a man possessed by a demon. Asked his name by Jesus, the man replied "Legion," referring to the many demons inside him. The demons begged Jesus to allow them to go into a herd of pigs feeding nearby. Jesus agreed, but as soon as the demons entered the pigs, the herd ran into the lake and drowned.

*A medieval ivory relief-carving shows a winged demon flying from the possessed man's mouth as some peaceful pigs gather on the left.*

*In this 14th-century work by Andrea Orcagna, Jesus (left, with his disciples) has just met Matthew and tells him to leave his money at the tax collector's booth.*

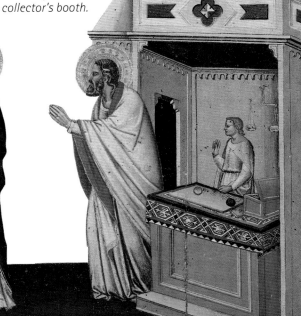

### THE CALLING OF MATTHEW, THE TAX COLLECTOR

After Jesus had left Gadarenes he saw a man named Matthew seated at the tax collector's booth. Tax collectors were despised in Jesus' time. They made profits by padding their accounts. Worse still, they mixed with Gentiles and worked on the Sabbath. Jesus addressed Matthew and called him to follow. Later Jesus dined at Matthew's house along with many tax collectors and other "sinners." Jesus later learned that the Pharisees had commented on this to the disciples. He said, referring to his ministry, "It is not the healthy who need a doctor, but the sick."

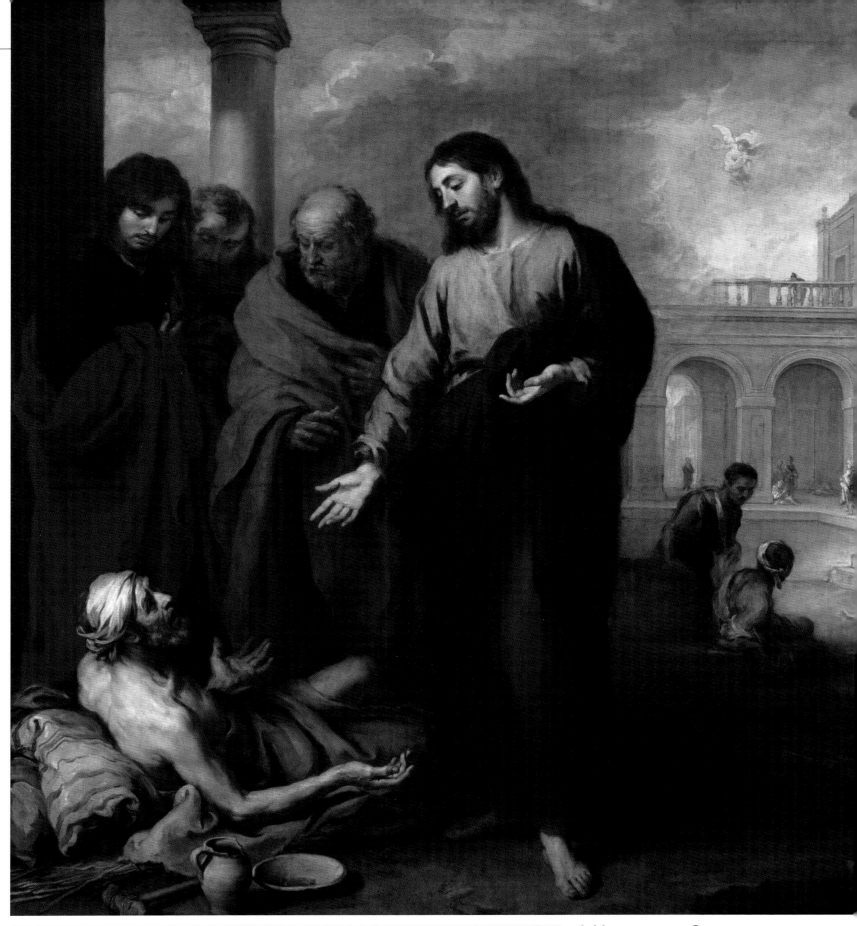

## JESUS HEALING THE PARALYTIC AT THE POOL OF BETHESDA
*Bartolomé Esteban Murillo*
c. late 1660s
The National Gallery, London (United Kingdom)

Bartolomé Esteban Murillo (1617-82) was a Spanish painter whose influence extended far beyond his native Seville. In this work he depicts Jesus (1) stopping to talk to the invalid (2). Peter (3) and two other disciples (4) listen to the man's story while, to the right a dog (5) (often included in scenes of the poor and sick) sniffs the ground. Beyond the dog are several other invalids (6) settling themselves into position by the edge of the pool. And above the pool is the angel (7), bathed in light and about to perform a miracle of his own.

## A MIRACLE ON THE SABBATH
John also reveals that this miracle occurred on the Sabbath, when Jewish law forbade work. That might explain Jesus' discreet behavior at the pool. Some religious authorities challenged Jesus as they had after his "blasphemous" forgiveness of sins (see page 9). Jesus replied that God — referred to as "My Father" — never stops working. These words infuriated the authorities, who saw them as blasphemous.

# The Pool of Bethesda

*Here a great number of disabled people used to lie – the blind, the lame, the paralyzed. One who was there had been an invalid for thirty-eight years. When Jesus saw him lying there..., he asked him, "Do you want to get well?" "Sir," the invalid replied, "I have no one to help me into the pool when the water is stirred. While I am trying to get in, someone else goes down ahead of me." Then Jesus said to him, "Get up! Pick up your mat and walk." At once. The man was cured; he picked up his mat and walked.*
John 5:1–9

John writes that while in Jerusalem, Jesus went to the Pool of Bethesda, where "crowds of sick people" gathered. An often omitted verse says how an angel, traditionally the archangel Raphael, would sometimes disturb the surface of the pool and the next person to enter the water would be cured of any illness. But the paralytic had never succeeded in being the first. Jesus asked whether the invalid wanted to be cured. The man replied that he simply wanted to be the first into the disturbed water. That was enough for Jesus to command the man to walk, and he did.

*Another treatment of the same subject by the Italian painter Giovanni Domenico Tiepolo (1727–1804) shows the archangel Raphael swooping down toward the water.*

*Below: The Dutch painter Jan Sanders van Hemessen (c. 1500–75) depicted the invalid carrying his mat away from the pool.*

### THE WOMAN WITH HEMORRHAGES

Jesus and his disciples left Gadarenes (see page 10) and crossed to the western shore of the Sea of Galilee. Among the crowd that met them was a synagogue official named Jairus. Jesus agreed to go and save Jairus' gravely ill daughter. Along the way, a woman suffering from hemorrhages (excessive bleeding) touched the fringe of Jesus' cloak, believing she would be cured. Jesus stopped and demanded to know who had touched him. Eventually, the woman came forward. Jesus said that her faith had healed her.

*Left: This detail from an early Christian painting from the catacombs in Rome shows the woman with hemorrhages kneeling to touch the hem of Jesus' cloak on the road to Jairus' house.*

# MIRACLE OF THE LOAVES AND FISHES
*Tintoretto*
c. 1580
Moss Stanley Collection, Riverdale-on-Hudson, New York (United States)

Paintings by the Venetian artist Tintoretto (1518–94), are often full of drama created by linking the figures in diagonal patterns and by balancing bright light with dark sections to highlight the miraculous subject matter of his work. In this painting, Jesus (1) is blessing the loaves and fishes held out by his two of his apostles, Philip (2) and Andrew (3). At the same time, Jesus gazes across at the young boy (4) who supplied the food. Two women watch from the right foreground. One of them is nursing a baby (5) who is too young to take part in the meal. On the hillsides beyond, and extending to the distance, are the 5,000 (6) who will be fed by Jesus.

# Multiplication of the Loaves and Fishes

*Jesus then took the loaves, gave thanks, and distributed to those who were seated as much as they wanted. He did the same with the fish....After the people saw the miraculous sign that Jesus did, they began to say, "Surely this is the Prophet who is come into the world."*　　John 6:11-14

Not long before the Jewish Passover Feast, Jesus led his disciples to a hillside on the far shore of the Sea of Galilee. A crowd of 5,000 followed them, having witnessed Jesus' miracles curing the sick. Toward the end of the day Jesus asked his disciples whether they could afford to pay for food for these people. Philip answered that it was impossible, but Andrew said that a young boy among them had five small barley loaves and two small fish. Jesus had the crowd sit on the grass. He gave thanks and distributed bread and fish to those who were seated. Jesus then had the disciples collect the leftovers, which filled 12 baskets.

### THE APOSTLES

Philip and Andrew played central roles in John's account of the Feeding of the 5,000. Both were among Jesus' first followers, and John describes Andrew (like his brother Peter, a fisherman) as the first of the disciples. Both of these men preached the Word after Jesus' death, and like Jesus, they were both crucified. European paintings of Philip and Andrew often depict them with a cross in recognition of the way in which they died. Andrew sometimes appears with a fishing net or a length of rope because he was tied, rather than nailed, to the cross.

### FEEDING THE HUNGRY

All four Gospels describe this miracle, although John's alone has Jesus giving thanks for, rather than blessing, the bread. The Greek word for giving thanks is "Eucharist," and the Christian Church came to use this word to describe the symbolic breaking of bread by the priest during the Mass. Later in John's Gospel, Jesus says "I am the Bread of Life." The fish is another potent symbol of Christ. The first letters of the Greek phrase *Iesous Christos theou hyios soter* ("Jesus Christ, Son of God, the Savior") spell *Ichthys*, the Greek word for fish.

*Left: A 5th-century mosaic from Ravenna, Italy. Jesus, arms outstretched, blesses the loaves and fishes while four of his disciples flank him.*

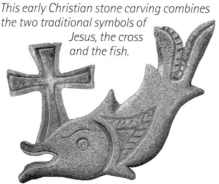

*This early Christian stone carving combines the two traditional symbols of Jesus, the cross and the fish.*

*This painting of Saint Andrew was executed in the mid-13th century by an anonymous artist working in the Italian town of Perugia.*

# Jesus Heals a Man Born Blind

*As he went along, he saw a man blind from birth.... he spit on the ground and made some mud with his saliva, and put it on the man's eyes. "Go," he told him, "wash in the Pool of Siloam." So the man went and washed, and came home seeing.* **John 9:6–7**

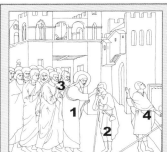

JESUS OPENS THE EYES OF A MAN BORN BLIND
*Duccio di Buoninsegna* panel from the *Maestà* c. 1308–11
National Gallery, London (United Kingdom)

The Siennese artist Duccio (c. 1255–1319) painted The *Virgin in Majesty* (the *Maestà*) for the high altar of Siena Cathedral. This panel is one of many scenes of Jesus' life that formed the back of the *Maestà*. It shows Jesus (1) applying the paste to eyes of the blind man (2), while the balding Peter (3) and other disciples watch intently. To the right is a second image of the blind man (4), just as he throws away his walking stick. The panel was originally next to a work of the Transfiguration, and the discarded stick would have drawn the viewer's eye to the image of the resplendent Jesus in the next panel.

While in Jerusalem, Jesus and his disciples met a beggar who had been blind since birth. Jesus told his disciples that no sin – either of the man or of his parents – had caused this blindness. Instead, the man was blind "so that the works of God might be revealed to him." Curing the man on the Sabbath enraged the Pharisees. They went on to reject the cured man when he refused to brand Jesus as a sinner.

### THE BLIND LEADING THE BLIND
Jesus used physical blindness as a metaphor for spiritual blindness — the inability to see the truth. The intransigent Pharisees, so often at odds with Jesus and scornful of his message, typified the spiritually blind. This symbolism underpins a famous parable in which Jesus says "If one blind man guides another they will both fall into the ditch."

*The Flemish painter Pieter Bruegel the Elder (c.1526–1569) takes the parable of the blind leading the blind and depicts it vividly in a Northern European setting of his time.*

### JESUS WALKS ON WATER
Matthew, Mark, and John tell of another "water miracle" that followed the feeding of the 5,000 (see pages 14–15). Jesus sent his disciples off by boat while he went to the hills to pray alone. That night Jesus came to the shore and saw the boat struggling against a headwind. He walked out on the water's surface toward the boat, reassuring the disciples. The wind died as Jesus entered the boat. Matthew extends the story to include Peter walking across to Jesus. Peter falters and is saved by Jesus, who reprimands him: "You have so little faith — why did you doubt?"

*Jesus saves a fearful Peter in this detail from a work by the 18th-century German artist Philipp Otto Runge.*

# The Raising of Lazarus

*Jesus called in a loud voice, "Lazarus, come out!" The dead man came out, his hands and feet wrapped with strips of linen, and cloth around his face. Jesus said to them, "Take off the grave clothes and let him go."* John 34:10-12

Jesus led his disciples from the Jordan River to Bethany, near Jerusalem, after he learned that his friend Lazarus was ill. Martha, Lazarus' sister, told Jesus that her brother had been in the tomb for four days. Jesus replied that Lazarus would live again because Martha believed that Jesus was the Son of God. He had the stone blocking the tomb removed and called out to Lazarus, who emerged from the tomb still wrapped in his burial clothes.

*In most depictions of the miracle, including this mosaic, Lazarus usually appears upright, in line with traditional Jewish burial practice.*

### LAZARUS EMERGES FROM THE TOMB

The story of Lazarus was differently interpreted by artists. Early paintings echo the words of the Bible and show Lazarus coming out of a cave tomb. Later treatments alter this somewhat, making the scene more familiar to Europeans themselves. In these works Lazarus is depicted coming out of a coffin, often set inside a building rather than a cave.

*Artists usually depict Mary Magdalene with her jar of expensive perfume which she used to anoint Jesus' feet, as in this 15th-century fresco by the Italian artist Piero della Francesca.*

### MARTHA AND MARY MAGDALENE

Lazarus' sisters feature strongly in the story of their brother. Martha, the practical sister, meets Jesus and says that Lazarus could have been saved if Jesus had arrived earlier. But she professes her faith in Jesus, paving the way for the miracle. Her sister Mary Magdalene is another loyal follower. She shows her faith when Jesus is a guest at their house by pouring expensive perfume on Jesus' feet and rubbing it in with her hair.

### THE RAISING OF LAZARUS
*Nicolas Froment*
1461
Uffizi Gallery, Florence (Italy)

Like many Italian and Flemish artists of the 14th and 15th centuries, the French painter Nicolas Froment (1435–86), took an interest in the often gruesome aspects of his subject matter. In this crowded work, the central figure is Jesus (1), blessing Lazarus (2) as he rises from the coffin. Martha (3) and Mary Magdalene (4) show their emotion, but Froment also shows Mary Magdalene holding a cloth to her nose to block the smell coming from someone who had been dead for four days. The disciples and other witnesses (5) stand before a row of golden arches (6) that are more in keeping with 15th-century Europe than with Judea at the time of Jesus. The young man (7) at the top left is believed to be a self-portrait of the artist Froment himself.

*Jesus blesses Martha while Mary Magdalene washes his feet in this work by the Siennese artist Duccio di Buoninsegna (c. 1255–1319).*

# The Healing of a Boy

THE TRANSFIGURATION
The event that immediately preceded the healing —
the Transfiguration — revealed Jesus' divine nature in
a dramatic way. Jesus took Peter, James, and John up

# The Haul of Fish

*Early in the morning, Jesus stood on the shore, but the disciples did not realize that it was Jesus. He called out to them, "Friends, haven't you any fish?" "No," they answered. He said "Throw your net on the right side of the boat and you will find some." When they did, they were unable to haul the net in because of the large number of fish.*   John 21:4–6

Fish would become a potent symbol of the Church. John describes the Haul of Fish as the last time the disciples saw Jesus after his resurrection. Peter, "the fisher of men" and a fisherman himself when he first met Jesus, led six of the others on a fishing expedition. Their bad luck changed once they followed the advice of the unknown person on the shore. John recognized him as Jesus and Peter immediately jumped off the boat to meet him. They later cooked some of the 153 fish they had caught. People at the time of Jesus believed there to be 153 species of fish. The number can represent the universality of the Church, and the unbroken net symbolizes the Church's capacity to contain everyone.

*This 14th-century crucifix by the Siennese painter Simone Martini captures the physical suffering of the crucified Jesus. Blood flows from Jesus' wounds as he breathes his last.*

*Below: This panel by Peter Paul Rubens vividly depicts one of the most famous of all gospel stories — that of Doubting Thomas, shown here examining Jesus' wounds.*

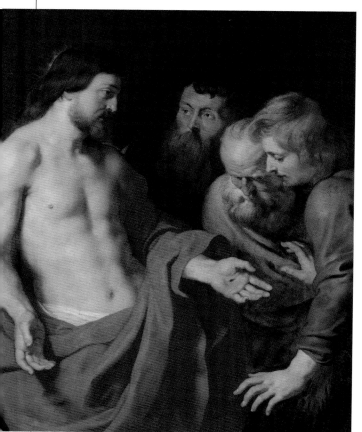

**THE DEATH AND RESURRECTION OF JESUS**
Jesus had drawn many followers during his few years of preaching, but he had also made many enemies. Chief among the enemies were the Pharisees, the strict interpreters of Jewish law who had criticized Jesus many times for breaking the Sabbath laws and — more importantly — for blasphemy in his references to his heavenly father. Jesus was crucified largely because of their influence. After three days, though, he rose from the dead and remained on Earth for 40 days before ascending into heaven. Proof of this Resurrection comes from the accounts of the disciples, who saw him during those 40 days.

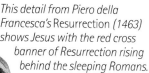

*This detail from Piero della Francesca's Resurrection (1463) shows Jesus with the red cross banner of Resurrection rising behind the sleeping Romans.*

## JESUS APPEARS TO HIS DISCIPLES

The gospels describe a number of instances when the resurrected Jesus appeared to the disciples. These meetings serve many purposes, but together they enable the disciples to understand the nature of Jesus' ministry and the nature of the redemption that Jesus' death had provided. Luke described two of the disciples walking on the road to Emmaus in the company of a stranger. They are downcast because they believe that a crucified Jesus could not have been the Messiah "to redeem Israel." The stranger (whom they eventually recognized as Jesus) rebukes them and explains how the Messiah's death had been foretold in the Scriptures. In other stories, the disciples cannot believe that the man they see is really the risen Jesus, returned in bodily form. The story of Doubting Thomas is the most familiar of these encounters, and it returns once more to Jesus' familiar theme of faith.

### THE MIRACULOUS DRAUGHT OF FISHES
*Konrad Witz*
1443–4
Musée d'Art et d'Histoire, Geneva (Switzerland)

Like his *Jesus Walking on the Waters*, this scene by Witz (1400–44) is as much a landscape of Lake Geneva as a biblical scene. It shows the disciples (1) hauling in a net that is nearly bursting with fish (2) while Peter (3) swims toward Jesus (4) on the shore. The disciples are clearly reflected in the lake water (5), but Jesus himself casts no reflection — an indication of his otherworldly existence after the Resurrection.

# The Descent of the Holy Spirit

*When the day of the Pentecost came, they were all together in one place. Suddenly a sound like the blowing of a violent wind came from heaven and filled the whole house where they were sitting. They saw what seemed to be tongues of fire that separated and came to rest on each of them. All of them were filled with the Holy Spirit and began to speak in tongues as the Spirit enabled them.        Acts 2:1–4*

In the miracle of Pentecost, the tongues of flame that came to rest on the assembly of Jesus' followers are a symbol of the burning power to speak out. The Holy Spirit — the third member of the Trinity after God the Father and Jesus — touched the disciples with this power to speak spread the message of good news and redemption that Jesus had proclaimed in his ministry.

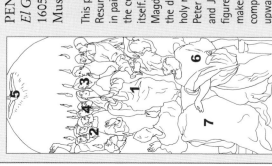

PENTECOST
*El Greco*
1605–1610
Museo del Prado, Madrid (Spain)

This painting by El Greco was almost certainly a pair to the Resurrection painted for the Colegio de Doña Maria. As usual in paintings of the Pentecost, it shows the Virgin Mary (1) in the center of the painting where she personifies the Church itself. She is surrounded by the 12 apostles (2), Mary Magdalene (3), and another pious woman (4). Above them, the dove (5) — symbol of the Holy Spirit — sends them its holy rays. At the bottom, kneeling in front of the Virgin, are Peter (6), considered the founder of the Christian Church, and John (7). As in many other paintings by El Greco, the figures are very long and, together with their gestures, makes them seem like flames themselves. This gives the composition vibrancy and creates the impression of an upward movement, or ascent.

## THE ASCENSION

The last time that Jesus appeared before his disciples was when he was taken up (ascended) to heaven in a cloud. This miracle occurred 40 days after Jesus' resurrection, and the period of 40 days has immense biblical significance. Jesus spent 40 days in the wilderness after being baptized, and in the Old Testament the 40-day period was crucial to stories of the Flood and the Exodus. Even the physical act of a body ascending into heaven had an Old Testament precedent with the story of Elijah. Significantly, the Holy Spirit descends upon the disciples after the Ascension. Jesus' bodily form had returned to heaven but the Holy Spirit would remain among God's people until the Day of Judgement.

# Peter

*One day Peter and John were going up to the temple at the time of prayer ... Now a man crippled from birth was being carried to the temple gate ... where he was put every day to beg from those going into the temple courts. When he saw Peter and John about to enter, he asked them for money ... Then Peter said, "Silver or gold I do not have, but what I have I give you. In the name of Jesus Christ of Nazareth, walk." Taking him by the right hand, he helped him up, and instantly the man's feet and ankles became strong.* **Acts 3:1–7**

Peter assumed the role of leader after Jesus ascended into heaven (see page 25), preaching in Jesus' name and performing miracles. In the Pentecost story, Peter addressed the skeptical Jews who believed that the apostles were drunk when they spoke in tongues, telling them that Jesus' mission had been foretold in the Scriptures. The healing of the beggar was the first of the miracles that Peter performed in his own ministry.

HEALING OF THE CRIPPLE
AND RAISING OF TABITHA
*Masolino da Panicale (and Masaccio)*
1425
Brancacci Chapel, Santa Maria del Carmine, Florence (Italy)

The Brancacci Chapel is a masterpiece of the early Renaissance. During the 1420s, the powerful Brancacci family commissioned the painters Masolino da Panicale (1383?–c.1440) and Masaccio (1401–1428) to paint a series of frescoes depicting biblical scenes, especially those relating to the life of Saint Peter. Their work displayed the new artistic sense of realism and perspective. This fresco concentrates on two of Peter's miracles. The left side shows the bearded Peter (1) extending his hand to help the beggar (2) get up and walk. The right side of the fresco depicts Peter (3) bringing the charitable woman Tabitha (4) back from the dead. Widows (5, 6) display clothes that Tabitha had made for them, while other companions look on in amazement.

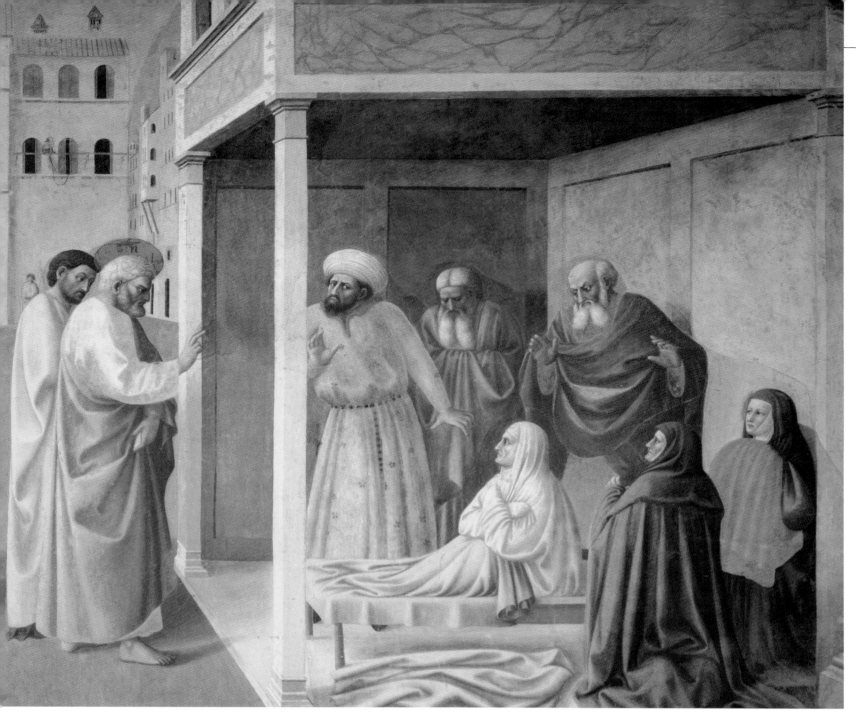

*A detail from a Sistine Chapel fresco by the 15th-century artist Pietro Perugino shows Jesus handing the "keys to the kingdom" to Peter.*

## PETER THE ROCK

Originally named Simon, Jesus' appointed leader was renamed Cephas. This Aramaic name appears in its Greek form Petros, or Peter (meaning "rock"), in the gospels. Jesus played with Peter's work as a fisherman and his name to spell out the important role he had in mind for him. "I will make you fishers of men," Jesus said to Peter and his brother Andrew. Peter had demonstrated his faith when he asked for the power to walk on the water like Jesus (see page 16). After Peter proclaimed Jesus as the Messiah at the town of Caesarea Philippi, Jesus said "On this rock (a play on Peter's name) I will build my community... I give you the keys to the kingdom of Heaven." After Jesus' ascension, Peter traveled and gained many converts to this community, or Church, despite being imprisoned several times. Tradition has it that he was crucified upside-down in Rome by the Emperor Nero in AD 64.

# The Conversion of Paul

*Meanwhile, Saul was still breathing out murderous threats against the Lord's disciples. He went to the high priest and asked him for letters to the synagogues in Damascus, so that if he found any there who belonged to the Way, whether men or women, he might take them as prisoners to Jerusalem. As he neared Damascus on his journey, suddenly a light from heaven flashed around him. He fell to the ground and heard a voice say to him: "Saul, why do you persecute me?"* Acts 9:1–4

*This image comes from an early 15th-century German representation of Paul's conversion. Jesus, accompanied by an angel, appears surrounded by light. The scroll reads: "Saul, why do you persecute me?"*

Although not one of the original 12 apostles, Paul is credited with being the first great Christian missionary to spread the faith to the Gentiles (non-Jews). He was born Saul to Jewish parents in Tarsus (now part of Turkey). Although Saul was a Roman citizen (and used the Roman name Paul), he was also a devout Jew who believed that the Christians were a threat to Jewish law and tradition. He was on his way to root out Christians in Damascus when he was blinded by the divine light.

## THE APOSTLES ARE PERSECUTED

More and more people had become Christians after hearing the apostles preach and witnessing their miracles. The Sadducees, strict interpreters of Jewish laws, were enraged and had the apostles imprisoned more than once. Stephen, a devout convert, became the first Christian martyr when he was convicted of blasphemy and stoned to death.

*This medieval Catalan painting shows Stephen (right) being stoned, his arms outstretched to meet those of God above him.*

THE CONVERSION OF SAINT PAUL
*Michelangelo Merisi da Caravaggio*
1600-01
Santa Maria del Popolo, Rome (Italy)

Caravaggio was a master of chiaroscuro, the dramatic use of light and dark in paintings. In this work, the bright light that highlights the fallen Paul (1) represents the light of the word — Jesus' message. Paul lies helpless while a companion (2) tries to calm his startled horse (3). The artist has painted the light in the same direction as the real light as it enters the church where the painting is found, adding a strong sense of reality. Caravaggio presents the scene as if he had just come across it in real life. There is no obvious evidence of God apart from the dramatic light. Even the focus of the painting, with the horse so prominent and the "main character" lying at the bottom, overturns the tradition of placing Paul in a central position.

## ANANIAS RESTORES PAUL'S SIGHT

Having been blinded by the light and fallen from his horse, Paul lay on the ground. Jesus spoke to him again, telling him to continue into Damascus where he would be told what to do. Paul's companions led him to a house in the city, where Paul fasted and prayed for three days. Meanwhile Ananias, a Christian living in Damascus, had a vision telling him to go to the house where Paul had been taken. When Ananias responded that Paul had persecuted Christians, Jesus told him that Paul had been chosen to spread the Christian message. Ananias went to the house and spoke about this message to Paul, who immediately regained his sight. Paul got up and was baptized by Ananias.

*This detail from a Greek icon shows a humble Paul being baptized by Ananias.*

# A Chronology of Miracles

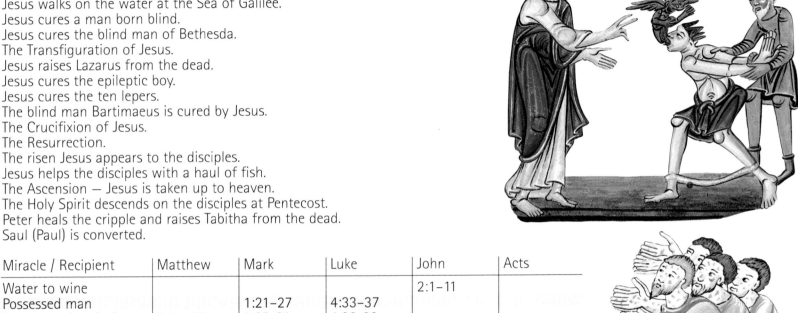

Jesus changes water into wine at the wedding in Cana.
Jesus cures a man possessed by a demon in Capernaum.
Peter's mother-in-law is cured by Jesus.
Jesus cures the leper.
Jesus cures the paralytic.
The servant of the faithful centurion is healed.
Jesus raises the son of the widow of Nain.
Jesus calms the Sea of Galilee.
Matthew, the tax collector, is called to be a disciple.
Jesus drives the demons possessing a man into a herd of swine.
A woman suffering from hemorrhages is cured after touching Jesus' cloak.
Jesus cures the invalid at the Pool of Bethesda.
The Miracle of the Loaves and Fishes.
Jesus walks on the water at the Sea of Galilee.
Jesus cures a man born blind.
Jesus cures the blind man of Bethesda.
The Transfiguration of Jesus.
Jesus raises Lazarus from the dead.
Jesus cures the epileptic boy.
Jesus cures the ten lepers.
The blind man Bartimaeus is cured by Jesus.
The Crucifixion of Jesus.
The Resurrection.
The risen Jesus appears to the disciples.
Jesus helps the disciples with a haul of fish.
The Ascension — Jesus is taken up to heaven.
The Holy Spirit descends on the disciples at Pentecost.
Peter heals the cripple and raises Tabitha from the dead.
Saul (Paul) is converted.

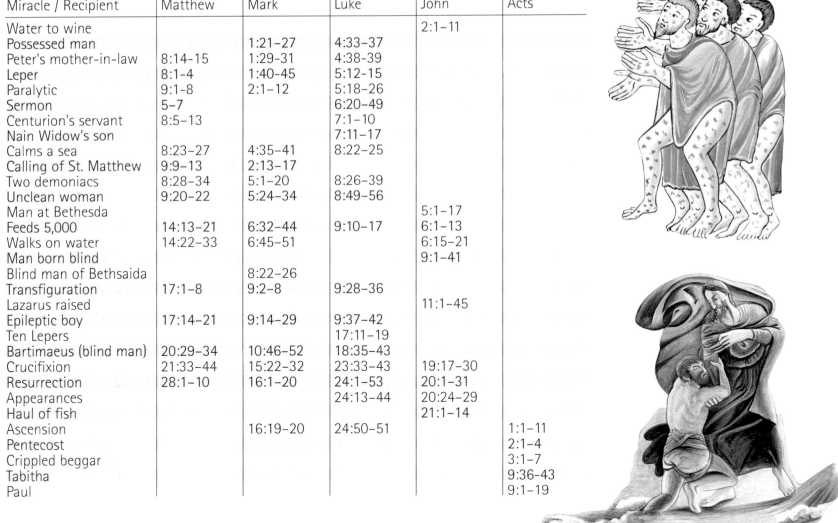

| Miracle / Recipient | Matthew | Mark | Luke | John | Acts |
|---|---|---|---|---|---|
| Water to wine | | | | 2:1–11 | |
| Possessed man | | 1:21–27 | 4:33–37 | | |
| Peter's mother-in-law | 8:14-15 | 1:29–31 | 4:38–39 | | |
| Leper | 8:1-4 | 1:40-45 | 5:12-15 | | |
| Paralytic | 9:1-8 | 2:1–12 | 5:18–26 | | |
| Sermon | 5–7 | | 6:20–49 | | |
| Centurion's servant | 8:5–13 | | 7:1–10 | | |
| Nain Widow's son | | | 7:11–17 | | |
| Calms a sea | 8:23–27 | 4:35–41 | 8:22–25 | | |
| Calling of St. Matthew | 9:9–13 | 2:13–17 | | | |
| Two demoniacs | 8:28–34 | 5:1–20 | 8:26–39 | | |
| Unclean woman | 9:20–22 | 5:24–34 | 8:49–56 | | |
| Man at Bethesda | | | | 5:1–17 | |
| Feeds 5,000 | 14:13–21 | 6:32–44 | 9:10–17 | 6:1–13 | |
| Walks on water | 14:22–33 | 6:45–51 | | 6:15–21 | |
| Man born blind | | | | 9:1–41 | |
| Blind man of Bethsaida | | 8:22–26 | | | |
| Transfiguration | 17:1–8 | 9:2–8 | 9:28–36 | | |
| Lazarus raised | | | | 11:1–45 | |
| Epileptic boy | 17:14–21 | 9:14–29 | 9:37–42 | | |
| Ten Lepers | | | 17:11–19 | | |
| Bartimaeus (blind man) | 20:29–34 | 10:46–52 | 18:35–43 | | |
| Crucifixion | 21:33–44 | 15:22–32 | 23:33–43 | 19:17–30 | |
| Resurrection | 28:1–10 | 16:1–20 | 24:1–53 | 20:1–31 | |
| Appearances | | | 24:13–44 | 20:24–29 | |
| Haul of fish | | | | 21:1–14 | |
| Ascension | | 16:19–20 | 24:50–51 | | 1:1–11 |
| Pentecost | | | | | 2:1–4 |
| Crippled beggar | | | | | 3:1–7 |
| Tabitha | | | | | 9:36–43 |
| Paul | | | | | 9:1–19 |

# Artists' Biographies

**Caravaggio** (born 1573 Caravaggio, died 1610, Porto Ercole, Grosseto) was born Michelangelo Merisi but took his professional name after the town of his birth. He was apprenticed in Milan to the painter Simone Peterzano, but worked in Rome from 1592. Caravaggio's early works were mainly small portraits and still-life paintings but from 1600 he entered a much bolder phase. With his choice of ordinary models, highlighted by luminarism (the strong contrast of light and dark), he completed a number of dramatic religious paintings. Caravaggio fled Rome in 1606 after killing a man in a brawl. He worked in Naples and then Malta and died of a fever while returning to Rome in search of a pardon.

**Duccio di Buoninsegna** (born c.1255, Siena, died c.1319, Siena) is considered the founder of the Siennese school. Little is known about his life and career. In 1308 Duccio received his greatest commission from the newly re-built Siena cathedral, the *Maestà* altarpiece. Duccio's style combined elements of Byzantine art (art of the Eastern Roman Empire, 330 ad – 1453 AD) with Italian medieval style. Duccio influenced generations of artists with his elegant, graceful style.

**Nicolas Froment** (born c. 1435, Uzès, died c. 1486, Avignon) spent his entire working life in his native Provence. He brought a sense of sculptural form to his paintings, which were nearly all commissioned for churches. His most famous work is the *Altarpiece of the Burning Bush* in the cathedral of Aix-en-Provence, which highlights his use of strong facial expression.

**El Greco** (born 1541, Candia, Crete, died 1614 Toledo) was known in Spain as "the Greek" because he was born on the island of Crete. His real name was Domenikos Theotocopoulos. Little is known of his Cretan youth, but by 1565 he was living in Italy where he was influenced by the work of Titian and Tintoretto. By 1577 he was working in Spain, on the huge altarpiece of the church of S. Domingo el Antiguo in Toledo. El Greco painted many great altarpieces and other works on religious themes, but was also renown as a portraitist. Beyond painting, El Greco is also recognized as a sculptor and architect.

**Károly Markó the Elder** (born 1791 Lócse, died 1860 Villa Appeggi) was a Hungarian painter who lived most of his life away from his homeland. Although he executed several paintings with religious themes, Markó was known mainly for his landscapes. His dramatic style, with its focus on natural grandeur, echoed that of contemporary Romantic painters such as the German Caspar David Friedrich. Markó's work was popular and from 1840 he had a comfortable existence based in Italy. Markó's three sons and one daughter also became painters.

**Masolino da Panicale** (born c. 1383, Panicale, died c. 1440, Florence) was born Tommaso di Cristoforo di Fini but used his birthplace near Florence as part of his professional name. He trained and began painting at a time when the Gothic style was still dominant but became influenced by Masaccio while the two worked together on Florentine projects in the 1420s. Under Masaccio's influence, Masolino began to experiment with perspective and the creative use of light and shadow, both hallmarks of the early Renaissance style.

**Bartolomé Esteban Murillo** (born 1618, Seville, died 1682, Seville) was one of the most famous Spanish painters of the 17th century. The naturalistic style of his early paintings, with their highly contrasting light and dark, gave way to a softer, warmer approach that tended to idealize the subjects. Murillo used this technique in a series of depictions of Franciscan saints as well as in several representations of The Immaculate Conception. Murillo had many followers and in 1660 he established an academy of art in Seville, becoming its first president. His death was probably the result of a fall from scaffolding while he was painting a *Marriage of Saint Catherine*.

**Rembrandt Harmenszoon van Rijn** (born 1606, Leiden, died 1669, Amsterdam) abandoned his university studies to pursue his art and by the age of 22 he had pupils studying under him. Even his earliest works show the maturity and power that led to his being recognized as the leading painter in Holland, if not all of Europe. Despite his public success, Rembrandt had a tragic private life. His wife and three of their four children died young. He overspent and was declared bankrupt in 1656, although he continued to work productively. Overall Rembrandt produced more than 600 paintings (including about 60 self-portraits), 300 etchings and 2000 drawings. About one-third of his output had a religious or biblical theme.

**Cosimo Rosselli** (born 1439, Florence, died 1507, Florence) was a successful painter whose reputation was built on his skilled draughtsmanship and high standard of craftsmanship rather than on any singularity as an artist. This competence, however, made him an excellent teacher and his pupils included the painters Piero di Cosimo and Fra Bartolommeo. His work in Florence includes frescoes in the Florentine churches of SS. Annunziata and S. Ambrogio. The high point of Rosselli's career was his being commissioned to paint frescoes on the walls of the Sistine Chapel, where he worked alongside Botticelli and Ghirlandaio.

**Tintoretto** (born c.1518 Venice, died 1594, Venice), whose real name was Jacopo Robusti, is known as one of the great painters of the late Renaissance and one of the last great Venetian masters. Tintoretto developed his style of by studying the works of Titian and Michelangelo. He became a famous painter in Venice and received many commissions from churches, religious groups, Venetian rulers, and the state. Three of his eight children became painters and assisted him in his workshop. Between 1564 and 1587 he painted his masterpiece, a series of biblical scenes on the ceilings and walls of the Scuola di San Rocco in Venice. He became an influential artist noted for his dynamic placement of figures and dramatic use of light.

**Paolo Veronese** (born 1528, Verona, died 1588, Venice), trained in his native Verona but lived in Venice from 1553 until the end of his life. He is considered, with Tiziano and Tintoretto, one of the greatest Venetian painters of the 16th century. In many of his paintings he portrays contemporary life in Venice, set magnificent architectural scenes. His works show an enormous talent for finding color harmony and clever use of perspective. During the 1560s he collaborated with the architect Palladio and the sculptor Vittoria in decorating the villas of Venetian noblemen. Veronese had a constant flow of commissions to produce religious and mythological works and he was aided by his large workshop, which included his brother and three of his sons.

**Konrad Witz** (born 1400, Rottweil, died 1444, Basel) came from Swabia (part of modern Germany) but spent most of his working life in the Swiss city of Basel. Like most artists of his time, Witz concentrated on religious subjects, producing a number of altarpieces and devotional paintings. His style was close to that of the Flemish painters Jan van Eyck, Rogier van der Weyden, and Petrus Christus, with whom he shared a liking for showing vast landscapes populated with tiny episodes drawn from everyday life and contemporary architecture. Many critics consider *The Miraculous Draught of Fishes*, with its depiction of Lake Geneva, to be the first European painting to portray an actual landscape rather than an idealized setting.

# Index

*Acts* 24, 26, 28
Ananias 28
Andrew 6, 14, 15, 27
Angelico, Fra 6
 – *Sermon on the Mount* 6
Apostles (see also Disciples and individual names) 4, 6, 14, 24, 26, 28
Beatitudes, the 6
Bethany 18
Branacci Chapel 26
Branacci family 26
Bridges, John 4
Bruegel, Pieter the Elder 16
Capernaum 4, 6, 9
Caravaggio, Michelangelo Merisi da 28, 31
 – *Conversion of Saint Paul* 28
Centurions 9
Cephas (see Peter)
Christians 28
Church 10, 15, 22, 24, 27
Colegio de Dona Maria 24
Damascus 28
Disciples 4, 6, 8, 10, 12, 13, 14, 15, 16, 18, 20, 21, 22, 23, 24, 25, 28, 30
Duccio di Buoninsegna 16, 18, 31
 – *Jesus Opens the Eyes of a Man Born Blind* 16
 – *The Virgin in Majesty* 16
Elijah 20, 25
Emmaus 23
Eucharist 15

Evangelists 4
Exodus 25
Flood 25
Froment, Nicolas 18, 31
 – *The Raising of Lazarus* 18
Gadarenes 10, 13
Galilee 4
 – Sea of 4, 10, 13, 15
Gentiles 9, 10, 28
Gospels 15, 22, 27 (see also John, Luke, Mark, Matthew)
Greco, El 24, 31
 – *Pentecost* 24
Heaven 26, 27
Hemessen, Jan Sanders van 13
Holy Land 9
Holy Spirit 24, 25
Israel 9, 10, 23
Jairus 13
James 6, 20, 21
Jerusalem 13, 16, 18, 28
Jesus
 – Ascension 25, 27
 – Baptism 4
 – Crucifixion 4
 – Ministry of 4, 23
 – Resurrection 22, 23, 24, 25
 – Transfiguration 16, 20, 21
Jews 4, 9, 21, 26
John, evangelist 4, 6, 12, 13, 15, 16, 18, 20, 21, 22, 24, 26
 – Gospel of 13, 15, 16, 22
John the Baptist 4

Jordan River 18
Judea 18
Judgement, Day of 25
Lake Geneva 23
Lake Tiberius 10
Luke 4
 – Gospel of 9
Mark 4, 16, 20
 – Gospel of 10
Markó the Elder, Károly 21, 31
 – *Healing of the Boy Possessed* 21
Martha 18
Martini, Simone 22
Mary (mother of Jesus) 24
Mary Magdalene 18, 24
Masaccio 26
 – *Healing of the Cripple and the Raising of Tabitha* 26
Masolino da Panicale 26, 31
 – *Healing of the Cripple and the Raising of Tabitha* 26
Mass 15
Matthew 4, 10, 16, 20
 – Gospel of 4, 6, 9, 20, 21
Messiah 23, 27
Miracles
 – Bethesda, Pool of 4, 9, 12, 13
 – Blind man, the 4, 16
 – Boy with a demon, the 20
 – Centurion's

servant, the 8, 9
 – Cripple, the 26
 – Demon-possessed man, the 10
 – Haul of fish, the 22
 – Jesus calms the sea 10
 – Jesus walks on water 4, 16
 – Lazarus, raising of 4, 18
 – Leper, the 4, 6
 – Multiplication of the loaves and fishes 4, 15
 – On the Sabbath (see Pool of Bethesda)
 – Paralytic, the 9, 13
 – Tabitha, raising of 26
 – Widow of Nain, son of the 8
 – Woman with hemorrhages, the 13
 – Wedding feast of Cana, the 4
Moses 20, 21
Mount Sinai 21
Murillo, Bartoleme Esteban 12, 31
 – *Christ Healing the Paralytic at the Pool of Bethesda* 12
Nain 8
Nazareth 6, 26
Nero, Emperor 27
Parables 6
 – The blind leading the blind 16
Passover Feast 15
Paul 28

 – Conversion of 28
Pentecost 24, 26
Perugia 15
Perugino, Pietro 27
Peter 4, 6, 12, 15, 16, 20, 21, 22, 23, 24, 26, 27
 – Ministry of 26
Petros (see Peter)
Pharisees 10, 16, 22
Philip 14, 15
Philippi, Caesarea 27
Piero della Francesca 18, 22
 – *Resurrection* 22
Piero di Cosimo 6
Raphael (archangel) 13
Raphael 20
 – *Transfiguration* 20
Ravenna 15
 – Church of Sant'Apollinare Nuovo 9
Red Sea 4
Rembrandt Harmenzoon van Rijn 10, 31
 – *The Storm on the Sea of Galilee* 10
Roman art
 – *The Miracles of Christ* 4
Roman Empire 9
Roman soldiers 8, 9
Romans 4, 9
Rome 4, 13, 27
 – Catacombs 13
Rosselli, Cosimo 6, 31
 – *Sermon on the Mount and the Healing of the Leper* 6

Rubens, Peter Paul 22
Runge, Philipp Otto 16
Sabbath 10, 12, 16
 – Laws 22
Sadducees 28
Saul (see Paul)
Scriptures 23, 26
Sermon on the Mount 6
Seville 12
Sienna Cathedral 16
Siloam, Pool of 16
Simon (see Peter)
Sistine Chapel 27
St Mark Basilica, Venice 10
Stephen 28
Syria 4
Tabitha 26
Tarsus 28
Thomas 22, 23
Tiepolo, Giovanni Domenico 13
Tintoretto 14, 31
 – *Miracle of the Loaves and Fishes* 14
Trinity 24
Veronese, Paolo 8, 31
 – *Jesus and the Centurion* 8
Witz, Konrad 23, 31
 – *The Miraculous Draught of Fishes* 23
 – *Christ Walking on the Waters* 23

# Acknowledgments

The Publishers would like to thank the following photographers and picture libraries for the photos used in this book.

Artothek, Spezialarchiv für Gemäldefotografie, Weilheim: 22-23

Corbis / Contrasto: 3 bottom, 12-13, 13 bottom right, 16-17, 26-27

The Bridgeman Art Library / Farabola Foto, Milan: 4 bottom left, 5, 11, 13 top right

The Picture Desk / Art Archive: 20-21

Scala Group, Florence: cover center, cover top right, 1, 6 center left, 7, 8-9, 9 bottom right, 10 bottom right, 14-15, 15 bottom right, 16 center, 18 top, 19, 20 bottom left, 22 bottom left, 24-25, 25, 28 center, 29